Furoshiki

The art of wrapping
with fabric

Kumiko Nakayama-Geraerts

Furoshiki

The art of wrapping with fabric

Kumiko Nakayama-Geraerts

NH
NEW
HOLLAND

Contents

Furoshiki, a Japanese art

Between history …

A furoshiki is a simple piece of cloth about one metre square in which objects of all shapes and sizes can be placed in order to carry them. There are many strong, elegant and ergonomic ways of folding the cloth that avoid the need to keep redoing the package. Furoshiki folding is an age old art. It was first seen in the Nara period (710–794) but has only really been established since the Kamakura period (12th–14th century).

Japan has experienced periods of conflict and instability in its history, periods when entire families travelled the roads from village to village looking for a peaceful place to stay. Between the 16th and 19th centuries the Tokugawa dynasty organized pilgrimages, like the pilgrimage of the eighty-eight temples of Shikoku, which could take several months. This life of constant movement brought with it the widespread use of folded and knotted fabric: the furoshiki. Later, merchants used furoshiki for carrying their goods, and also to decorate them. So figures depicted in prints are often seen carrying their possessions on their back, wrapped in large furoshiki. Today furoshiki are still part of everyday life for the Japanese: they are used for carrying shopping and school books, for wrapping up winter futons, and so on.

The word itself evokes another tradition, *furo* bath and *shiki* carpet, suggesting that furoshiki were used to carry and store personal belongings at the public baths.

… and tradition

A furoshiki is far more than simple packaging; it goes hand in hand with the art of giving gifts. In Japan, offering a gift is not a matter of simple politeness, it is a strong gesture with a real symbolic, traditional and ceremonial element. One learns very early on never to give an unwrapped gift: everyone learns to carry a gift at chest height to show its worth, however great or small. The gift is not only the object inside the wrapping but also the wrapping itself and the way in which the gift is given. Very few Japanese would offer a present wrapped just in paper. The art of folding a furoshiki is an integral part of social life in Japan.

When a young girl is given her first kimono she must take great care of it. She learns very quickly to wrap the kimono and accessories up in a furoshiki, as all women do. The kimono is a precious garment, also steeped in history and tradition, so it goes without saying for all Japanese that it should be folded away in a furoshiki.

Furoshiki in everyday use

An gesture both ecological …

Countries the world over are increasingly preoccupied with ecology and the protection of the environment: many laws and government actions have been introduced to limit pollution. For this reason the Japanese Minister for the Environment, Yuriko Koïke, is strongly promoting the return of the furoshiki. Moreover furoshiki boutiques are now appearing in large numbers, and courses in folding techniques are available.

Neglected in favour of plastic bags in an era of plentiful oil, the furoshiki tradition is now experiencing a revival, linked with the desire to limit the use of non-recyclable packaging. When we know that a plastic bag takes around 400 years to biodegrade, isn't it more respectful to use a square of cotton or linen each time you go shopping? When it gets dirty you just wash it and use it again, whereas a plastic bag gets torn and is thrown away after use.

… and elegant

Furoshiki are multipurpose; you can put anything in them. Isn't is more elegant to carry your lunch in a furoshiki rather than a bag advertising a shop (even a famous one)? A furoshiki can easily replace a shopping bag, a suitcase, a box and even a rucksack. Furoshiki come in many different colours, plain, in two colours or patterned. However some colours are traditionally reserved for special occasions: in Japan the same furoshiki is never used for both a wedding and a funeral! For example for weddings, a furoshiki with the family emblem is used. But for everyday use anything is permissible.

Women in Japan use Kyoto-style furoshiki, sophisticated patterned fabrics in pastel shades, and men use Edo-style furoshiki, in darker colours like brown or emerald green. We are even starting to see furoshiki created by young designers that appeal to adolescents and young adults. Naturally, when you come to

> To go even further you can use soap nuts. These are the fruits of the *Sapindus Mukorossi*, a tree that grows in India and Nepal. They have been used for centuries as a washing product. The shell of the nut contains a cleaning substance, saponin, which acts like natural soap in contact with water (see p.64).

create your own furoshiki you will be free to choose the colours you find most suitable. You can also personalize them with embroidery, small bells, etc.

The furoshiki is now an essential accessory for anyone who cares about the environment and style.

Make your own furoshiki

Although some folding styles are codified by Japanese tradition according to use, you will soon understand that you can use a furoshiki to wrap any object for any occasion. So as you gain experience you will adapt the style to the object in question. You can easily hold a guitar case in a large furoshiki by combining the folding technique for bottles with the rucksack technique.

 Easy

Intermediate

Difficult

Sizes

The furoshiki is always square in shape. It comes in different sizes, depending on the volume of the object to be wrapped. As your technique becomes more refined over time you will make several furoshiki for different occasions. These are the traditional sizes of furoshiki:

Small furoshiki (45 or 50cm) are used for wrapping snacks or lunch. Made of synthetic silk, they are also used in Japan for wrapping money for special celebrations.
Medium-sized furoshiki (68 or 75cm) are the most popular. Made of cotton or synthetic fabric, they are used to wrap gifts to present when visiting someone.
Large furoshiki (90 or 105cm) are used every day for wrapping bottles and carrying shopping. The 105cm size is an ideal container for shopping, bottles and even personal items for a weekend away. We recommend that you start with this size as it is the most versatile.
Very large furoshiki (110 or 130cm) are often made of cotton. They are used for wrapping cushions and clothes before they are stored away in a cupboard.
The giant size furoshiki (175, 200 or 230cm) is also often made of cotton. It is used for storing large items like futons and for moving house.

🌸 Small

🌸🌸 Medium

🌸🌸🌸 Large

Take it even further and use fair trade fabrics.

Fabrics

Two types of fabric are used for furoshiki: attractive material for gifts and rather less sophisticated fabric for carrying things.

Stronger cotton- or linen-based material is preferable for carrying things, but of course it's up to you if you want to use synthetic or denim fabrics.

The Japanese use plain or patterned furoshiki made of silk to wrap presents, very often with each side a different colour.

Don't be afraid to personalize your furoshiki. Embroidery (like the examples shown at the end of the book), pompoms, pearls, mirrors… any personal touch you can think of – the scope for creativity is enormous. Let your imagination run free!

  Strong fabric

  Fabric for gifts

Perfect finishes

To obtain a strong and elegant fold your furoshiki must have good finishes. This is a simple way to achieve a perfect hem.

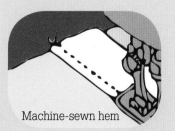
Hand-sewn hem

It is advisable to sew hems by hand because the stitches are then invisible. Turn the fabric down by about 1.5cm. Turn the edge of the hem under and tack it 1.25cm from the fold. Then finish the hem using slip stitch: insert the needle just below the hem and slide it under the hem fold. Continue for the length of the hem.

You may also choose to use a sewing machine for the hem, but the finish will be less satisfactory. This method should therefore be avoided for a furoshiki to be used for a gift.

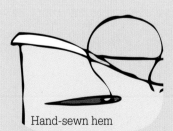
Machine-sewn hem

Knots

The knots shown here are the four basic knots for furoshiki folds. They are all as strong as each other and can be used indiscriminately. Make your choice according to preference or the purpose of the wrapping.

Square knot

1. Make a single knot by crossing the right end over the left end. Then wrap the right end around the left end and pass it through the hole formed. The two sides have thus crossed over and you have the first knot.

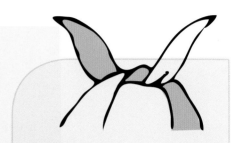

2. Cross the two ends over again and pass the right one beneath the left.

3. You then have two knots, one sitting above the other.

4. Pull them tight with the two ends lying in the same direction as the fabric, ie horizontally.

Vertical square knot

1. Make a single knot by crossing the right end over the left end. Then wrap the right end around the left end, and pass it through the hole formed. The two sides have thus crossed over and you have the first knot.

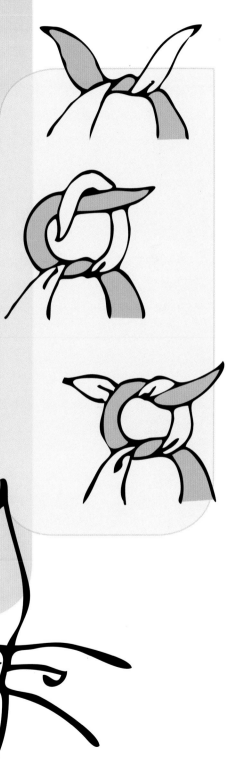

2. Cross the two ends over again and pass the right one over the left.

3. You then have two knots, one sitting above the other.

4. Pull them tight with the two ends lying in the opposite direction to the fabric, ie vertically.

Butterfly knot

1. Make a single knot by crossing the right end over the left end. Then wrap the right end around the left end and pass it through the hole formed. The two sides have thus crossed over and you have the first knot.

2. Form a loop with the right end.

3. Pass the left end around the loop. Form a second loop with the left end and push it through the hole formed.

4. Pull the loops tight to make a butterfly (or loop) knot .

14

Single loop knot

1. Make a single knot by crossing the right end over the left end. Then wrap the right end around the left end and pass it through the hole formed. The two sides have thus crossed over and you have the first knot.

2. Form a loop with the right end.

3. Pass the left end around the loop. Push the left end through the hole formed.

4. Pull tight to make a knot with a single loop.

Folds for carrying

The following furoshiki folding techniques will enable you to carry objects of different shapes and sizes anywhere. Choose the most appropriate style for your needs.

Ball fold and variation

1. Spread the furoshiki out wrong side up and place your items in it.

2. Fold the furoshiki in half diagonally and tie the two corners that meet in a knot.

3. Tie a knot in the third corner half way down so the items do not fall out.

4. Tie the fourth corner in a knot and carry the furoshiki by the handle thus formed.

Variation

1. Spread the furoshiki out right side up. Fold it in half diagonally.

2. Tie a knot in the two corners that are not touching.

3. Turn the furoshiki inside out. The knots will be inside and the right side will be outside.

4. Tie the remaining two corners together in a knot.

Katakaké fukuro

Ball fold with handle

1. Spread the furoshiki out wrong side up and place your items in it.

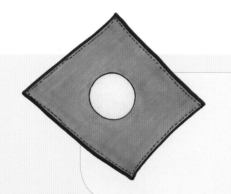

2. Knot the two left corners together. Do the same with the right corners.

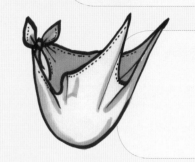

3. Pass one knotted end through the other.

4. Take hold of the lower end. The other will take care of itself. This furoshiki is very handy for bulky objects.

Suika tsutsumi

Knapsack or shoulder bag

1. Spread the furoshiki out wrong side up and place your items in it. Make a single knot to hold the items in place.

2. Tie these two corners again using a square knot or vertical square knot.

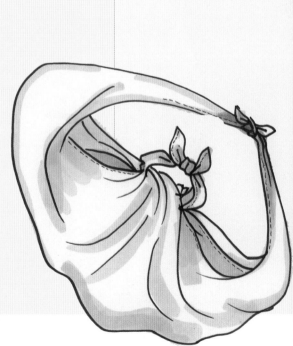

3. Knot the two remaining corners to create a large handle. Carry the bag over your shoulder or across your back.

Variation

Repeat step 1 but make a square knot. Knot the two remaining corners to create a handle. In this way you can easily make a shoulder bag.

Nanamegake musubi

Wrapping a square or round dish

1. Spread the furoshiki out wrong side up and place your covered dish in it.

2. Fold the top corner inwards and form into long pleats.

3. Take the right corner to the left behind the pleats, crossing it over the front of the dish. Do the same with the left corner: take it to the right behind the pleats, crossing it over the front of the dish. Tie the left and right corners in a knot behind the pleats. The dish is then enclosed and all that remains is the front corner.

4. Tie the last corner in a knot close to the dish.

Kashibako tsutsumi

Carrying a book

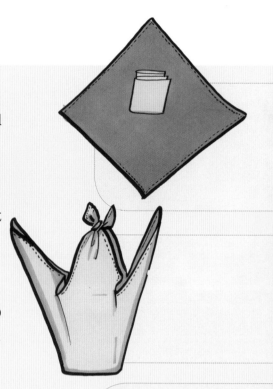

1. Spread the furoshiki out wrong side up and place your book in it.

2. Fold the furoshiki diagonally and knot together the two corners that meet.

3. Stand the book up. Cross the remaining two corners in front and wrap them around the book.

4. Knot the two corners together at the back.

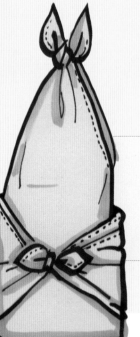

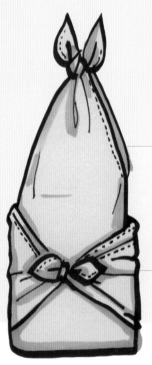

Carrying two books

1. Spread the furoshiki out wrong side up. Place the two books near the left and right corners of the furoshiki. Fold the corners over the books.

2. Roll the books towards the centre of the furoshiki. Leave a small space between the two books.

3. Fold the bottom corner towards the top. Fold the top corner towards the bottom. You still have two corners free and the books are covered.

4. Close the fold by putting one book on top of the other and tie the two remaining corners. This will give you a handle to carry the books with.

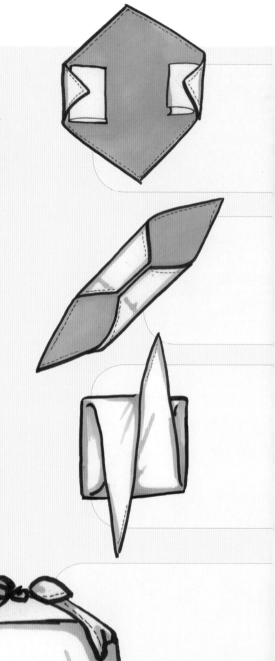

Hon tsutsumi

Carrying a bottle

1. Spread the furoshiki out wrong side up. Stand the bottle up in the centre of it.

2. Fold the furoshiki diagonally and tie the two corners that meet in a knot.

3. Cross the two remaining corners over the front.

4. Tie the two remaining corners together at the back.

Carrying two bottles

1. Spread the furoshiki out wrong side up. Lay the two bottles down in the centre with the necks facing the corners. Leave a space between the two bottles.

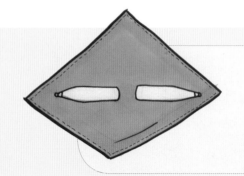

2. Bring the bottom corner up over the bottles.

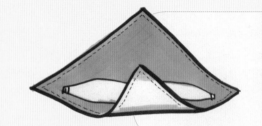

3. Roll both the bottles towards the top, making a tube.

4. Stand the bottles up side by side. Tie the two remaining corners in a knot.

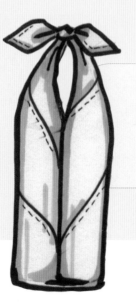

Rabbit-shaped fold

1. Spread the furoshiki out wrong side up. Place the apple in the centre.

2. Fold the furoshiki diagonally.

3. Roll up the two corners and tie them in a knot. Pull them out to look like ears.

4. Knot the two remaining corners below the rabbit's head using a square knot.

5. Tuck the corners inside the knot to look like paws.

Folds for wrapping

A gift, yes … but one wrapped in a furoshiki! The following folding methods save on wrapping paper and are much more original. Be sure to personalize your furoshiki in keeping with the occasion.

Square box

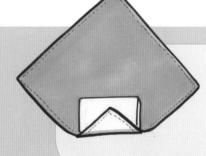

1. Spread the furoshiki out wrong side up. Place the box near the bottom edge and roll the corner over it.

2. Roll the box in the furoshiki.

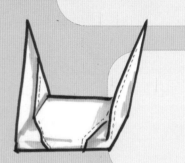

3. Fold the two remaining corners over the box; cross them over twice and take them underneath.

4. Tie the corners in a knot underneath.

Sao tsutsumi

Square box with one corner underneath

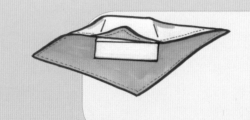

1. Spread the furoshiki out wrong side up. Place the box in the centre. Fold the top corner over the box.

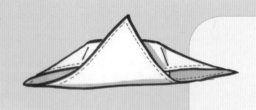

2. Fold the bottom edge over the box, making sure that the corner extends beyond it.

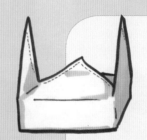

3. Lift up the two side corners.

4. Knot the two side corners over the top of the box allowing the corner of fabric below to show.

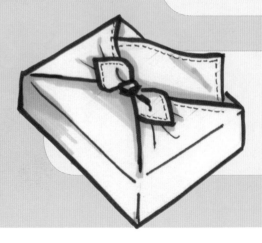

Otsukai tsutsumi

Square box with one corner on top

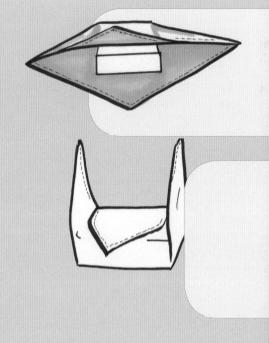

1. Spread the furoshiki out wrong side up. Place the box in the centre. Fold the top corner over the box.

2. Fold the bottom edge over the box, making sure that the corner extends beyond it. Lift up the two side corners.

3. Knot the two side corners over the top of the box.

4. Pull the corner out from under the knot and lay it over the top.

Kakushi tsutsumi

Square box with four knotted corners

1. Spread the furoshiki out wrong side up. Place the box in the centre.

2. Knot two corners diagonally over the box.

3. Fold the other two ends over the box.

4. Make the same knot with the other two corners, underneath the first knot.

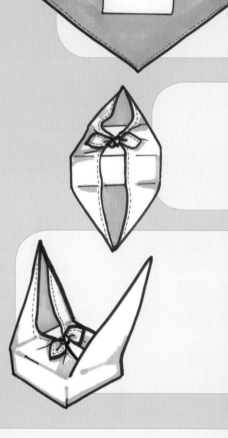

Long Box

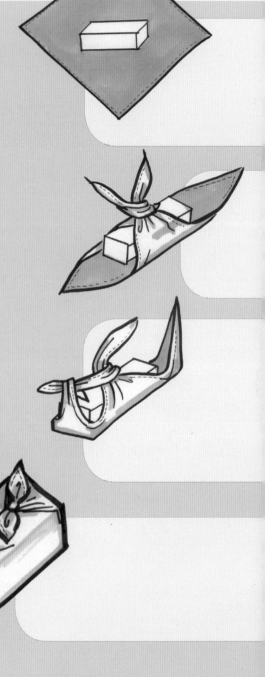

1. Spread the furoshiki out wrong side up and place the box in the centre.

2. Wrap the two diagonal corners of the furoshiki around each other.

3. Wrap the front corner around the left corner and the back corner around the right corner.

4. Tie a knot where the corners meet.

Futatsu tsutsumi

Box with flower-shaped knot on top

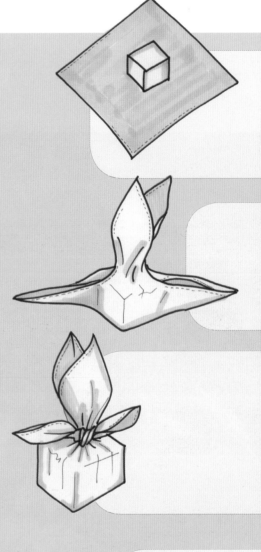

1. Spread the furoshiki out wrong side up and place the box in the centre.

2. Lift the two diagonal corners up over the box.

3. Wrap the two side corners around the first two corners and tie them in a knot. Allow the ends to fall loose.

4. Insert the two free ends into the knot, making folds to imitate a flower.

Hana kazari fukuro

49

Flower in a pot

1. Spread the furoshiki out wrong side up. Place the pot in the centre. Fold the bottom corner up so the fold is the same height as the pot. Do the same with the top corner.

2. Wrap the other two corners around the pot.

3. Tie the corners with a single loop knot, allowing the longest end to hang down.

Flower bouquet

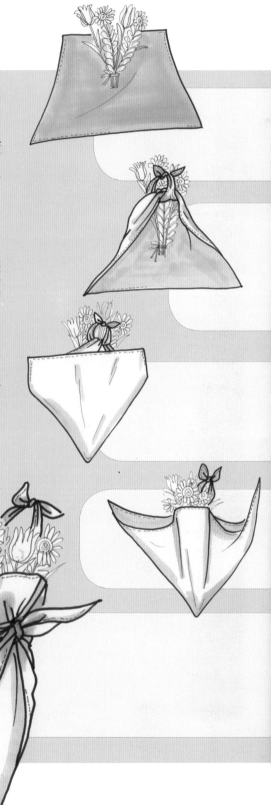

1. Spread the furoshiki out wrong side up. Place the bouquet in the middle of the top half of the furoshiki, allowing the flowers to extend beyond the top edge.

2. Tie the two top corners over the flowers using a single knot and then a square knot to create a handle.

3. Fold the bottom half of the furoshiki up over the stems.

4. Turn the bouquet over. Fit the furoshiki around the stems.

5. Tie the two remaining corners around the bouquet.

Hana bukuro

Bottle

1. Spread the furoshiki out wrong side up. Lie the bottle down in the centre.

2. Fold the bottom half over the bottle and then the top half.

3. Stand the bottle up. Tie the two corners behind the bottle.

4. Roll the two ends up.

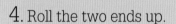

5. Wrap the two ends around the bottle and secure the corners so that the fold does not come undone.

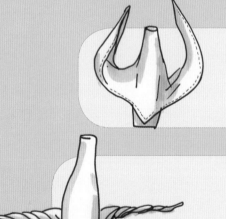

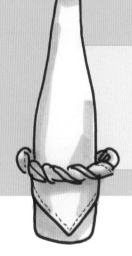

Embroidery designs

The following embroidery designs have been specially created to enable you to personalize your furoshiki. You can easily adapt them to suit your preferences. Let your imagination loose!

Sashiko

Sashiko is a traditional style of Japanese embroidery found on 11th-century prints, but it can also be found in the fashion magazines of today. It usually consists of white stitching on indigo blue fabric.

1. For a furoshiki with sides of 105cm, make a sashiko 51cm square

2. Trace your design and transfer it onto the centre of the furoshiki.

3. From the centre, follow the lines of the pattern using running stitch. Take care that the stitches do not touch each other at the point where the lines cross.

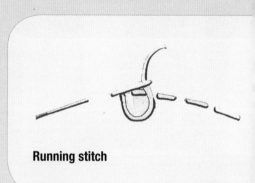

Running stitch

4. Smooth the fabric out regularly. This technique is called *itoshigoki*.

5. When you have finished the embroidery, iron the fabric on the reverse using a warm iron.

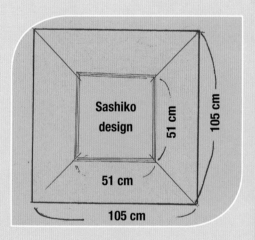

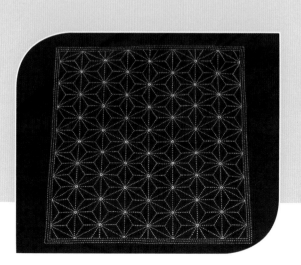

Frogs and rabbits

These frogs and rabbits are inspired by the *Chô-jûgiga*, scrolls painted by the monk Toba showing anthropomorphic animals playing and frolicking. The scrolls date from the 12th century and are now kept in the Tokyo National Museum.

1. These sizes are ideal for a furoshiki 100cm square. Draw a diagonal line and divide it into four sections.

2. Trace the frogs and rabbits and transfer them onto the fabric, two on either side of the diagonal line, towards the corners and two on the line, nearer the middle.

3. Embroider the designs using stem stitch.

4. Iron the furoshiki on the reverse with a warm iron.

Stem stitch

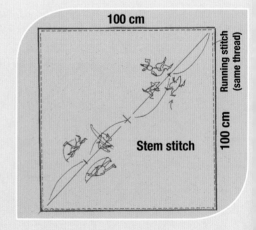

100 cm

100 cm

Running stitch (same thread)

Stem stitch

Stylized flowers

These flowers are an original and modern design ideal for long folds. The embroidery and appliqué techniques are included here.

1. These designs will fit a furoshiki 103cm square. Draw a diagonal line and mark the centre point.

2. Trace the designs and transfer them onto one half of the furoshiki, joining the stems in the centre. Leave approximately 23cm between the corner of the furoshiki and the tallest flower.

3. Embroider the stems using back stitch, running stitch and chain stitch.

4. Fill the flowers in with fabric appliqués: cut out the desired shape in a different fabric, position it where you want it and sew it on.

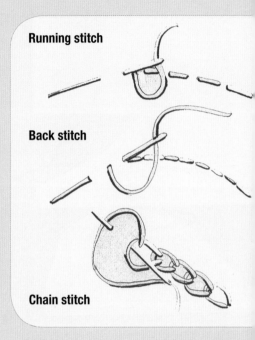

Running stitch

Back stitch

Chain stitch

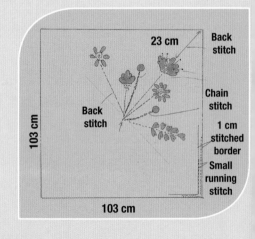

23 cm

Back stitch

Back stitch

Chain stitch

1 cm stitched border

Small running stitch

103 cm

103 cm

Where to find traditional furoshiki

www.etsy.com
www.thejapaneseshop.co.uk
www.ebay.co.uk

Where to find soap nuts

www.ecotopia.co.uk
www.inasoapnutshell.com

Acknowledgements

The author wishes to thank Agathe, Solène and Jean-Luc.
The editor wishes to thank the models for their kind participation: Cécile, Colinda, Madeleine, Alexis,
Thibaut and shoppers in the Aligre market. Thanks also to the Baron rouge and to Jérôme and all the team
in the bookshop La Manæuvre.

First published in 2011 by
New Holland PUblishers (UK) Ltd
London ▪ Cape Town ▪ Sydney ▪ Auckland

Garfield House
86–88 Edgware Road
London W2 2EA
United Kingdom
www.newhollandpublishers.com

80 McKenzie Street
Cape Town 8001
South Africa

Unit 1, 66 Gibbes Street
Chatswood, NSW 2067
Australia

218 Lake Road
Northcote, Auckland
New Zealand.

This book was designed and produced by:
Éditions Tutti Frutti
28 rue Sedaine
75011 Paris – France
www.tuttifrutti.fr

Text, photos and drawings © 2008
  Un Dimanche Après Midi
Éditions Tutti Frutti is a registered
trademark of Un Dimanche Après Midi

10 9 8 7 6 5 4 3 2 1

ISBN : 978-1-84773-816-5
English translation © 2011 New Holland Publishers